poems of Gloria Darlene Mann

GLORIA MANN

CALLING FROM

SAN FRANCISCO,

CALIFORNIA

Writings herein are the product of Gloria Darlene Mann, and she is responsible for the contents. Wider Perspectives Publishing reserves 1st run rights of this work and all rights revert to the author upon delivery. Author then reserves the right to grant or restrict reprinting of this volume in whole or in part and may resubmit for contests and anthologies at will.

Copyright Gloria Mann, 2019
August 2019, San Francisco by way of Hampton Roads, Va./ Wider Perspectives Publishing
1st edition ISBN: 9781690814443
2nd edition June 2020 ISBN: **978-1-952773-08-2**

I didn't know anything of Gloria Mann until she was mentioned to me by a mutual friend during a discussion on poetry. She recommended that I take a look at some of Gloria Mann's work and was confident that I would like what I saw. When I got to peruse the pieces that she had on hand I came to realize that, in this poetry, I was getting a clearer view of the writer's soul than I had encountered at any other time. While she addresses diverse topics and her poetic style takes on a couple of different voices, her soul speaks consistent and presents a certain clarity.
She was right, Ms. Mann's work and my publishing work are a good match.

– J. Scott Wilson, Poet, author of <u>Fist in the Air, Heart on the Ground</u>, publisher, editor

Whether standing up for Matthew Shepard and the "people of the world today whose spirits are crucified on the fence of secrecy, of 'Don't ask, Don't tell,'" or standing up for herself – surviving a childhood like walking through a minefield detonating all around me," and teaching herself to breathe again, the poems of Gloria Mann are deep, courageous, and touch the heart. Extending forgiveness to a formerly violent parent – caring for her with tenderness and love, and "...the day she discovered common sense was uncommon... she saw the real magic was to be clearly, thoughtfully, intentionally, completely present," the spirituality and kind voice of Gloria Mann comes through like a warm hug and makes an old friend of each new reader.

– Judith Stevens, Poet

Contents

- *Breathe* — 2
- *The Gift* — 4
- *For Matthew Shepard* — 6
- *Sacred Space* — 8
- *Joy* — 10
- *Sleepwalker* — 12
- *The Myth of "Me"* — 14
- *Gossip* — 16
- *Speed Bumps* — 18
- *Emotional Rape* — 20
- *Infinity* — 22
- *Archie* — 24

BREATHE

Cradled in warm water
Soft as a baby's breath
I rock in my safe world
Until I'm ready to emerge into the universe.

Childhood like walking through a minefield
Detonating all around me
It was here that I first learned to hold my breath
Held my breath in panic
Braced against a world racked with Fear.

Today, in small glimmers of hope, I learn the world is once
       More safe again
Holding my breath now separates me
When every moment is precious
So I learn to breathe again
Like an infant awakening to life
Breathe
Remember to breathe
Like water running through a brook,
Like trees swaying in the earth,
Remember to breathe.

THE GIFT

When my father suddenly died in 1985
I was the one who moved in to take care of mom
Mother who made childhood a nightmare
Mother whose tenderness was punctuated by extreme violence.

I decided to make room for the heart.
I wanted to dive into mom's ocean of sickness
and emerge full of understanding
grasping what had made her the way she was.
I got much more. There was the mom who, now old and helpless,
Had come full circle to be a child again.
Jewels of tenderness filled her soul as we drank hot chocolate together,
looked at pictures of both our childhoods and exchanged expressions
of love.

This was much more than I bargained for.
Forgiveness is the pearl for which we all must dive,
If we want to be truly alive.

FOR MATTHEW SHEPARD

It was your intention in life
To fight for the underdog
You had a thirst for justice
Which made it so tragic for all of us
That you were brutally beaten
And then left to die tied to that split-rail fence
In the remote outskirts of Laramie, Wyoming.

It is small consolation to us to know
That as you were on the verge of crossing over
You were looking at the beautiful starlit sky of Laramie
      that you loved so much Matthew.
You were Mother Earth's tender child
You saw spirit everywhere
And with an open heart
You embraced everyone.

Even as you struggled to survive
You brought people together
As gay and straight people alike marched through
      the streets of Laramie on your behalf
While you lay in the hospital bed still
      Clinging to life.

And it was in your death that the first Hate Crime
    Legislations were sparked all across this country.
Once again, through you were no longer with us,
You brought out the best in us.

May all the LGBT people of the world today
Whose **spirits** are crucified on the fence
    Of Secrecy,
    Of "Don't ask, Don't tell",
    Of Let's throw all the transgenders out of the
military
Be inspired by your courage Matthew
We will never forget you and what happened to you.

I want October 12, 1998
The day your light was extinguished
To become A Day of Remembrance.
May we rewrite the world
To be a world where it is safe for everyone
To be who they truly are.

SACRED SPACE

Words wisp through the air like dragonflies
Making a symphony of sound
Disturbing noises no longer imprison them
And a marvelous symphony of music abounds.

Cigarette smoke no longer strangles me
Leaving words gasping for air
Poems are no longer left dangling
Choking for expression, in mid air.

The search for solitude is a writer's dream
This sudden silence stirs my soul
Quiet space is needed to create a poem
Where all the pieces come together to make a whole.

Sacred space yields sacred art
It evolves into a treasure
It is filled with a healing light
And that is above all measure.

JOY

The sun rising
Children giggling on a playground
Dew on the windshield
Everything counts
When the universe is sacred.

SLEEPWALKER

She liked the world vague
It's why she didn't wear her glasses
That hazy overtone soaked through
With such magical mystery

She reached for her first drink
To drown the voices of fear
To drown a world she didn't understand anymore
A world filled with murdered leaders,
Dying causes,
Republicans
&
The Religious Right.

In the solitary confinement of her head
Where people rented space and didn't pay a thing
She couldn't touch
     feel
          connect
               stand up
                    Walk a straight line

But there was no magic
Just a blur passing out from one day to another
Until the day she discovered common sense was uncommon.

That day the booze and drugs went down the drain.

And she saw the real magic
Was to be cleary,
    Thoughtfully,
        Intentionally,
            Completely present.

THE MYTH OF "ME"

Me is not the answer
Me is not the way
In fact in my experience it will lead you quite astray.

We are all connected
We are all the same
If we want to feel genuine love
We must do it in all our names.

Community is the answer
Community is the key
It is only there that we will find true life gains.

In a world based on self
people starve and people cry
But when all the wealth is at the top 3%
I don't wonder why.

Even pop psychology has given it a try
But building **self** esteem will not bring you joy
Because we are all connected
And anything else is a ploy.

Give me a world where all our relations have respect
and I'll give you a world that is the best yet.
Brothers and sisters we all are
It's of no use being a self-centered star.

GOSSIP

To gossip is to kill a soul
First the other's, then one's own
It will never make you whole
It will burn inside you like a stone.

Gossip is a way to feel superior
Competing all the while you make someone inferior
While doing it you don't have to see your own flaws
Perhaps that is the real cause.

There's nothing more damaging to community
then picking on someone to achieve immunity
If you want to be able to look at yourself in the mirror
Do behavior that will bring people near.

To criticize only creates separation
The real challenge is cooperation -
It bridges the invisible distance between us all
Which never really existed in the first place, after all.

SPEED BUMPS

Racing through my life riddled with Fear
careening out of control
Nothing can stop me I think,
wholly directed by self-will
I slam into a Speed Bump
and I'm knocked back into my senses.

Prayer slows me down and takes me to the
very core of existence
The Center of Me
The Center of all that is.

Slower still is meditation
The sweetness of that white light stirs my soul,
rocking me back and forth
into a world where Fear has no place
where movin' too fast doesn't fit
Running away no longer works
Running from what
From whom
to where?

Where it will take you is running head-long into a
Speed Bump
where I'm reminded once again
to slow down.

Grace has a position in this universe
and it has been Grace all along
protecting the souls of the Earth.

There is no longer a place for "fight or flight" in this
new universe
A world filled with Love and Serenity.
Grow in peace.
Grow in justice.
Grow in grace.

EMOTIONAL RAPE

To not be believed
Is like having your body dragged over hot coals
Unprotected
Unnurtured
People who drag degrees behind their name
    Can be dangerous
They think they know everything
No humility
No teachability
They victimize the victim a second time
And think nothing of it
I pull myself out of the fire
I put on sacred clothing
I call in the Ancestors
I surround myself with healing light
I join the universe as a Warrior,
Ready to do battle for what is Right.

INFINITY

I walk out to the warmest stretch of sand,
Staring at the wide expanse of sea,
And I am contemplating Death.

If there's an afterlife
I'll be back
But if there isn't
There will never be a trace of me again.
What a frightening thought.

I prefer to think
No one can get it right
The first time around
So we come back many times
To learn the important lessons about love and life
Line upon line,*
Stone upon stone,*
Until we know how to love and live with one another.

When we do we ascend in a blazing glory of light
To join the stars
To merge with a universe
That has always understood we are all interconnected

And we will finally understand the infinity of relationship,
    Never Random,
        Pregnant with meaning,
            Bursting with insight.

*Edgar Cayce

ARCHIE

(In the 1930's & 40's, there was a cartoon strip called "Archie and Mehitabelle", about a cockroach named Archie and his romance with Mehitabelle the cat. I was inspired by the cartoon to name this poem "Archie".)

Today I found a cockroach in my room
He was slow and dim-witted, so I didn't make him leave too soon.
Just a poor critter trying to come in from the cold
My guess, too, is that he was quite old.

I named him Archie
and imagined him a poet
jumping from key ro key
writing love poems to whoever knows it.

After all him and his friends been here longer than us,
Since the time of the dinosaurs
And I wonder what magical things they discuss.

Cockroaches even thrive on nuclear radiation
What a wonder that is
They exceed us in cooperation
While our world is in such a tiz.

So I take my hat off to Archie
I will do him no harm
The meek shall inherit the earth
While we're still triyng to figure out how to disarm.

Colophon
Brought to you by Wider Perspectives Publishing, care of James Wilson, with the mission of advancing the poetry and creative community of Hampton Roads, Virginia.
See our production of works from …

Tanya Cunningham
    (Scientific Eve)
Terra Leigh
Ray Simmons
Samantha Borders-Shoemaker
Taz Waysweete'
Bobby K.
    (The Poor Man's Poet)
J. Scott Wilson (TEECH!)
Zach Crowe

Charles Wilson
Jorge Mendez & JT Williams
Sarah Eileen Williams

Stephanie Diana (Noftz)
the Hampton Roads Artistic Collective
Jason Brown (Drk Mtr)
Martina Champion
Tony Broadway
Ken Sutton
Crickyt J. Expression

… and others to come soon.

We promote and support poetic artists
  from the seats, from the stands,
  from the snapping fingers and clapping hands
  from the pages, and the stages
  and now we pass them forth to the ages

Check for the above artists on FaceBook, the Virginia Poetry Online channel on YouTube, and other social media. Hampton Roads Artistic Collective is the non-profit extension of WPP and strives to simultaneously support worthy causes and the creative artists.

www.ingramcontent.com/pod-product-compliance
Lightning Source LLC
LaVergne TN
LVHW041313080426
835510LV00009B/969